On The
First Christmas Day

John M. Chilson

A story to be read aloud at Christmas time,
or any time of the year,
to children of all ages who look at the
night sky in wonder
and hear the angels singing:
"Glory to God in the Highest and Peace on Earth."

On The First Christmas Day

This is the home edition:
and is available on Amazon.com.
There is also an 11–inch by 8.5–inch
spiral bound Storyteller Edition.
Both editions are available
at www.NorthPoleMarketing.com/books.

ISBN-13: 978-1533330895
ISBN-10: 1533330891

Dedicated to my grandchildren,
my great–grandchildren to come
and all the children of the world.
I pray they will love this story as much as I do
and that they will share it with their children.

A very special "Thank You" to two wonderful women
whose help made this story better...
Darlene Chilson, my wife, and
Deloris Giltner, friend and editor.
Without their help I would have kept struggling
for a long time and probably still not got it right.

On The First Christmas Day

Introduction

How do you tell children the story of the birth of Jesus so that they will make a connection between the star on the top of their Christmas Tree and the Star of Bethlehem? That is the problem I am hoping this little book will help solve. Read it aloud and sing the chorus or all the verses. Have fun with it.

Storyteller ideas

The entire song may be sung to the common "Happy Birthday" tune. You might sing the chorus every time you turn a page or have a different person or group sing each verse.

Consider pausing at the end of each page and asking questions or calling attention to something that is happening in the story or picture.

In the poem, the name "**Jesus**" is in red. Whenever you come to it, pause, point to the children and let them say His name.

For the full story of the birth of Jesus, please read Luke chapters 1 and 2 in the Bible.

On The First Christmas Day

Tune "Happy Birthday", Traditional
Lyrics by John M. Chilson

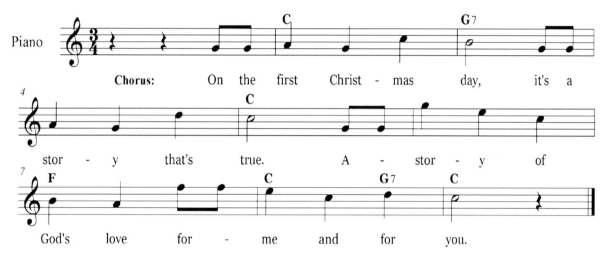

Chorus: On the first Christ - mas day, it's a stor - y that's true. A - stor - y of God's love for - me and for you.

On The First Christmas Day

Chorus:
"On the first Christmas Day,"
it's a story that's true.
A story of God's love for me and for you.

1) It was a long time ago, almost three thousand years,
   when the prophet named Micah
   said to all who would hear:

2) "Little town of Bethlehem, you will give us a King.
   a great man who will save us,
   and his praises we will sing."

3) Many long years later all the people still worried.
   but God is never late and God is never hurried.

4) Then God told Isaiah and Isaiah told us,
   "A baby will be born, his name will be **Jesus**."

On The First Christmas Day

5) Many more years later a new baby was born,
   when God's time was right,
   on a dark winter morn.

6) With the donkeys and camels was born a baby boy.
   He was God's son,
   named **Jesus**,
   for all a great joy.

7) Mary wrapped him up tight,
   in a blanket he lay.
   She fed him,
   then placed him in a bed made of hay.

On The First Christmas Day

8) When **Jesus** was born,
   a new star in the night appeared over the stable
   with a very bright light.

9) In the fields there were shepherds
   watching over their sheep.
   The night was very cold;
   and the darkness was deep.

On The First Christmas Day

10) When suddenly an angel appeared to them all.
"Do not be afraid,
I bring good news for all.

11) "In Bethlehem town is a new baby boy,
to all of God's people He brings great joy.

12) "He is the Savior;
his name is **Jesus**.
From all of our sins only he can save us."

13) "You will know by this sign when you find him today:
Wrapped warm in a blanket in a manger of hay."

On The First Christmas Day

14) Then the sky was soon filled with angels so bright.
    They sang praises to God in that cold and dark night:

15) "Glory to our loving God in the highest heaven,
    and peace on earth to all men and women."

On The First Christmas Day

16) When the angels had gone,
    to town the shepherds went.
    and found the small stable where they had been sent.

17) Wrapped warm in a blanket, the baby was there.
    They knelt down and worshipped this child small and fair.

On The First Christmas Day

18) Another group soon came;
    they'd traveled from afar.
    They were wise men, maybe kings, who had followed the star.

19) They entered the stable with presents they'd brought;
    gold, frankincense and myrrh
    for the child whom they sought.

On The First Christmas Day

20) So remember this child when you celebrate Christmas,
the day **Jesus** was born and God's best gift to us.

21) Put a star on your tree
and a few angels too.
Think on that first Christmas
and God's gift to you.

Chorus:
"On the first Christmas Day,"
it's a story that's true.
A story of God's love for me and for you.

Made in United States
North Haven, CT
20 December 2022

29869180R00015